Scrambled Sentences
WORD FAMILIES

40 Hands-on Pages That Boost Early Reading & Handwriting Skills

Snake will make another cake.

Snake will make another cake.

New York • Toronto • London • Auckland • Sydney
Mexico City • New Delhi • Hong Kong • Buenos Aires

Written and produced by Immacula A. Rhodes
Cover design by Tannaz Fassihi
Interior design by Jaime Lucero
Cover and interior illustrations by Doug Jones

ISBN: 978-1-338-11302-0

3 4 5 6 7 8 9 10   40   23 22 21 20 19 18

Contents

Scrambled Sentences Activity Pages

Introduction

Welcome to Scrambled Sentences: Word Families!

The 40 activity pages in this book were developed to give children an engaging and fun way to practice recognizing word families and to put words together to create, read, and write sentences. In addition to boosting early reading and writing skills, the activities also give children lots of opportunities to hone their fine motor and visual skills.

On each page, children cut out and unscramble a set of words to create a sentence that describes a picture. The sentence includes words that belong to a specific word family, giving children repeated practice in recognizing and reading those words. Once children have arranged and glued the words into a sentence, they write that sentence on the provided line and then color the picture. As they do the activity, children perform a number of tasks, such as cutting, gluing, writing, and coloring, which help build and strengthen their fine motor abilities.

You can use the scrambled sentences with the whole class, in small groups, or as the focus of a one-on-one lesson. You can also place them in a learning center for children to use independently or in pairs. The activities are ideal for children of all learning styles, ELL students, and for RTI instruction. And best of all, they support children in meeting the standards for Reading Foundational Skills for grades K–2. (See below.)

Connections to the Standards

Print Concepts
Demonstrate understanding of the organization and basic features of print.

Phonics and Word Recognition
Know and apply grade-level phonics and word analysis skills in decoding words.

Phonological Awareness
Demonstrate understanding of spoken words, syllables, and sounds (phonemes).

Fluency
Read with sufficient accuracy and fluency to support comprehension.

Source: © Copyright 2010 National Governors Association Center for Best Practices and Council of Chief State School Officers. All rights reserved.

How to Use the Scrambled Sentences

Materials (for each child)

- scrambled sentence page
- scissors
- glue
- pencil
- crayons

Completing a scrambled sentence page is easy and fun. To begin, distribute copies of the activity page for the word family you want to teach. Point out the words that target that skill on the page and read them aloud. Then have children do the following:

 1 Cut out the word strip at the bottom of the page. Then cut apart the words.

 2 Put the words in order to make a sentence that goes with the picture. Glue the words in the sentence box.

 3 Write the sentence on the line.

4 Color the picture.

Note: *See the Scrambled Sentences List on page 7 to check the correct word sequence for the sentence on each activity page.*

Teaching Tips

Use these handy tips to ensure children get the most from the scrambled sentence activities.

- **Provide a model:** Display a completed scrambled sentence page. Then demonstrate, step by step, how to complete the activity, including the use of think-alouds to model how to figure out individual words and the sentence.

- **Focus on the target word family:** Have children identify each of the words that belong to the target word family, read the word aloud, and color the word. In addition, ask them to find and name the items in the picture that belong to the target word family. Point out that many of the images picture additional things that belong to that word family.

- **Use the clues:** Point out that children can use the picture to help figure out individual words and what the sentence should say. They can also use what they know about sentence features to sequence the words: The first word of a sentence begins with a capital letter and the last word ends with a punctuation mark.

- **Reinforce reading at every step:** Have children read each word after cutting apart the words, before and after gluing the words in place, and after writing the sentence. As children read the sentence, encourage the use of an appropriate inflection for that type of sentence (statement, question, exclamation).

Scaffolding Suggestions

Provide support as children's needs dictate. Here are a few suggestions.

Reading

- Display each word and help children sound it out. You might also read the word aloud and have children repeat.

- Point out each word that belongs to the target word family and ask children to read the word aloud, repeating it several times.

- Provide the correct word order for the sentence. As needed, work individually with children to put the sentence together, one word at a time.

- Model reading the sentence aloud and have children repeat.

Writing

- Have children practice writing the words that belong to the target word family on the line, instead of the full sentence. If needed, write the words on the line in advance and have children trace them.

- Ahead of time, lightly pencil in the sentence on the writing line. Then have children trace the sentence.

TIP

For children with less developed cutting skills, cut out each individual word in advance. Or cut out the word strip and have children cut apart the words.

Ways to Use the Scrambled Sentences

- Learning center activity
- Whole-class instruction
- Small-group instruction
- One-on-one lesson
- Partner activity
- Individual seatwork
- Morning starter
- End-of-the-day wrap up
- Take-home practice

More Uses

- Label a folder with each child's name. Encourage children to place their completed scrambled sentence pages in their folder. Have children use the pages for review and to practice reading.

- Help children compile their pages into a booklet to take home and share.

Customized Scrambled Sentences

Use the template on page 48 to create your own scrambled sentences. First, choose a word family to feature on the page. Print the word-family ending in the box at the upper-right side of the page. Then create a sentence that features words that belong to the identified word family. For best results, limit the word count to six or fewer words and the total letter count to 22 or fewer letters. Draw a simple sketch to represent the sentence and write the words in random order on the strip at the bottom of the page. (Be sure to include a capital letter for the first word of the sentence and punctuation with the last word.) Separate the words with vertical cutting lines, leaving space between each one. Then copy a class supply of the page to distribute to children.

Scrambled Sentences List

Use this handy list as a reference for checking the correct word sequence for the sentence on each activity page.

-ab *(page 8)*
Crab tries to grab the cab.

-ack *(page 9)*
Jack has to pack his snack.

-am *(page 10)*
Pam eats jam on her ham.

-ell *(page 11)*
The bell fell into the well.

-en *(page 12)*
Hen left her pen at ten.

-et *(page 13)*
My pet just met the vet.

-ig *(page 14)*
Pig wears a very big wig.

-ing *(page 15)*
The king loves to swing!

-ip *(page 16)*
Skip puts his chip in dip.

-og *(page 17)*
Frog hops onto a log.

-ot *(page 18)*
This spot got really hot!

-ox *(page 19)*
Fox drops toys into the box.

-ub *(page 20)*
Cub plans to scrub the tub.

-ump *(page 21)*
Duck can jump over the stump!

-unk *(page 22)*
Skunk keeps junk in the trunk.

-ail *(page 23)*
Snail goes to get the mail.

-ain *(page 24)*
The rain fell on our train.

-ake *(page 25)*
Snake will make another cake.

-ale *(page 26)*
Dale found a whale on sale.

-ape *(page 27)*
Ape used tape on her cape.

-ay *(page 28)*
Jay likes to play in hay.

-each *(page 29)*
Each girl can reach a peach.

-eam *(page 30)*
We all dream of ice cream!

-eep *(page 31)*
Two sheep sleep in a jeep.

-ice *(page 32)*
The mice think rice is nice.

-ike *(page 33)*
Mike can ride a bike!

-ive *(page 34)*
Five bees drive to the hive.

-oat *(page 35)*
Goat can float like a boat.

-one *(page 36)*
That phone looks like a bone.

-ose *(page 37)*
Mom chose the big rose.

-ow *(page 38)*
Crow likes to play in snow.

-ue *(page 39)*
Sue takes the blue glue.

-all *(page 40)*
The small ball hit a wall.

-ark *(page 41)*
Clark needs to park his shark.

-ew *(page 42)*
Drew blew his new whistle.

-irt *(page 43)*
Kim had dirt on her shirt.

-ook *(page 44)*
A fish shook my hook.

-ouse *(page 45)*
Mouse ran into the house.

-own *(page 46)*
Clown wore a crown to town.

-oy *(page 47)*
Roy gives the boy a toy.
OR: Roy gives a boy the toy.

Name _____

-ab

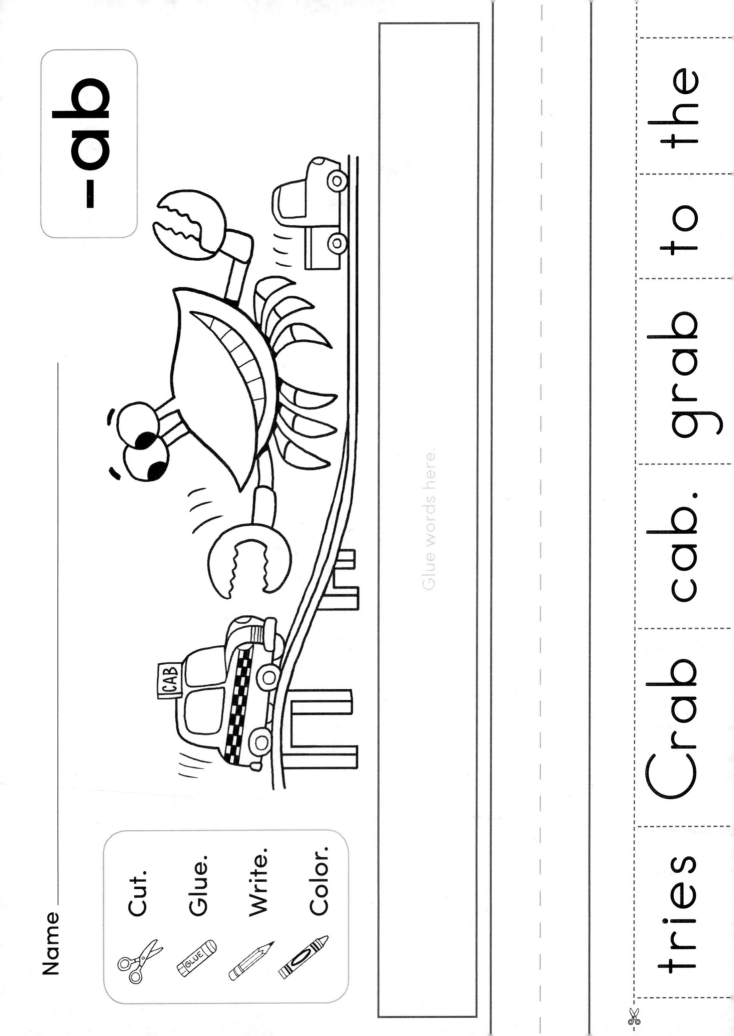

Cut.

Glue.

Write.

Color.

Glue words here.

tries   Crab   cab.   grab   to   the

-ack

Cut.

Glue.

Write.

Color.

Glue words here.

snack. has his to Jack pack

Name _____

-am

Cut.
Glue.
Write.
Color.

Glue words here.

✂ on | her | Pam | eats | ham. | jam

Name _____

-ell

Cut.   ✂
Glue.   GLUE
Write.   ✏
Color.   🖍

Glue words here.

The   fell   bell   the   into   well.

Name _____

-en

Cut. ✂

Glue. 🗒GLUE

Write. ✏

Color. 🖍

Glue words here.

---

her | ten. | pen | Hen | at | left

Name _____

-et

WELCOME
TO THE
PET VET!

Cut. ✂
Glue. 🖊GLUE
Write. ✏
Color. 🖍

Glue words here.

the   met   just   vet.   pet   My

-ig

Name _____

Cut.

Glue.

Write.

Color.

wears | Pig | wig. | very | a | big

Name _____

-ing

Cut.
Glue.
Write.
Color.

Glue words here.

king	swing!	loves
loves	swing!	king
The	to

-ip

Name _____

Cut.
Glue.
Write.
Color.

BEST CHIPS EVER

CHIP DIP

Glue words here.

in   his   Skip   puts   chip.   dip

Name _____

-og

Cut.
Glue.
Write.
Color.

Glue words here.

Frog | onto | hops | log. | a

-ot

Name _____

Cut.
Glue.
Write.
Color.

Glue words here.

got | really | This | hot! | spot

Name _____

-ox

Cut.

Glue.

Write.

Color.

Glue words here.

TOY BOX

the   into   toys   box.   drops   Fox

Name _____

-ub-

Cut.
Glue.
Write.
Color.

Glue words here.

plans | Cub | tub. | scrub | to | the

Name _____

-ump

Cut.

Glue.

Write.

Color.

Glue words here.

stump! | can | the | jump | Duck | over

Name _____

-unk

Cut.

Glue.

Write.

Color.

Glue words here.

in   the   Skunk   keeps   trunk.   junk

Name _____

-ail

Cut.
Glue.
Write.
Color.

SNAIL
125

Glue words here.

Snail to goes the get mail.

-ain

Name _____

Cut. ✂

Glue. 🗒GLUE

Write. ✏

Color. 🖍

ZOO TRAIN

Glue words here.

fell | train. | on | The | our | rain

Name _____

-ake

Cut.
Glue.
Write.
Color.

Glue words here.

Snake | will | make | another | cake.

Name _____

-ale

Cut.
Glue.
Write.
Color.

SALE

STUFFED TOYS

Glue words here.

found | Dale | sale. | whale | a | on

found | Dale | sale. | whale | a | on

Name _____

-ape

Cut.
Glue.
Write.
Color.

Glue words here.

cape. | used | her | tape | Ape | on

-ay

Name _____

Cut.
Glue.
Write.
Color.

Glue words here.

play   in   Jay   likes   hay.   to

Name _____

-each

Cut.
✂

Glue.
GLUE

Write.
✏

Color.
🖍

Glue words here.

peach.

reach

a

girl

can

Each

✂

Name _____

-eam

Cut. ✂️

Glue. 🖍️

Write. ✏️

Color. 🖍️

Glue words here.

dream cream! of We ice all

Name _____

-eep

ZZzz

PEEP!

Cut. ✂

Glue. 🖊GLUE

Write. ✏

Color. 🖍

Glue words here.

a   in   sleep   jeep.   sheep   Two

Name _____

-ice

Cut.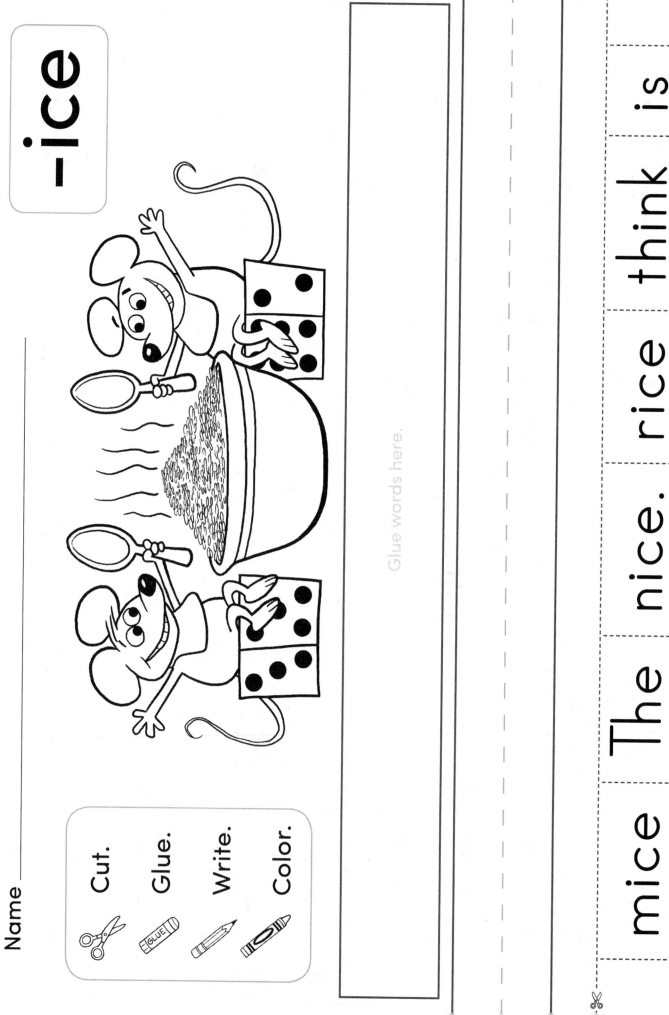
Glue.
Write.
Color.

Glue words here.

mice The nice. rice think is

Name _____

-ike

Cut. ✂
Glue. 🖊GLUE
Write. ✏
Color. 🖍

Glue words here.

can bike! ride Mike a

Name _____

-ive

HIVE
SWEET
HIVE

Cut.

Glue.

Write.

Color.

Glue words here.

to   the   Five   bees   hive.   drive

Name _____

-oat

Cut. ✂

Glue. 🖍

Write. ✏

Color. 🖍

Glue words here.

Goat float can a like boat.

-one

Name _____

Cut.

Glue.

Write.

Color.

Glue words here.

looks | bone. | like | That | a | phone

Name _____

-ose

Cut. ✂

Glue. GLUE

Write. ✏

Color. ▬

Glue words here.

rose. | big | the | chose | Mom

-OW

Name

Cut.
Glue.
Write.
Color.

Glue words here.

likes   Crow   snow.   play   to   in

Name _____

-ue

Cut.
Glue.
Write.
Color.

GLUE SALE TODAY!

WHITE RED GREEN YELLOW ORANGE BLUE

Glue words here.

takes   glue.   the   Sue   blue

Name _____

-all

Cut. ✂
Glue. GLUE
Write. ✏
Color. 🖍

Glue words here.

hit a The small wall. ball

Name _____

-ark

Cut.

Glue.

Write.

Color.

PARKING

Glue words here.

Clark   to   needs   his   park   shark.

Name _____

-ew

Cut. ✂
Glue. 🖊
Write. ✏
Color. 🖍

Glue words here.

---

his | new | Drew | whistle. | blew

✂

Name _____

-irt

Cut. ✂
Glue. 🖊 GLUE
Write. ✏
Color. 🖍

Glue words here.

✂

| her | on | dirt | shirt. | had | Kim |

Name _____

-ook

Cut.
Glue.
Write.
Color.

Glue words here.

fish A my shook hook.

Name

-ouse

Cut.
Glue.
Write.
Color.

Glue words here.

ran   house.   into   Mouse   the

Name _____

-own

Cut.

Glue.

Write.

Color.

TOWN

Glue words here.

crown   to   Clown   wore   town.   a

Name _____

-oy

Cut. ✂

Glue. 🖊

Write. ✏

Color. 🖍

Glue words here.

Roy the gives a toy. boy

Name

Cut.
Glue.
Write.
Color.

Glue words here.